Cow Way

with *Isle of Bute*

Michael Kaufmann
and
James McLuckie

Rucksack Readers

Cowal Way: with Isle of Bute

Second edition published in 2016 by Rucksack Readers, 6 Old Church Lane, Edinburgh, EH15 3PX, UK, comprehensively revised from the original edition published by Rucksack Readers in a different format in 2009.

Telephone   +44/0 131 661 0262

Website   *www.rucsacs.com*

Email   info@rucsacs.com

Distributed in North America by Interlink Publishing, 46 Crosby Street, Northampton, Mass., 01060, USA (*www.interlinkbooks.com*)

British Library cataloguing in publication data: a catalogue record for this book is available from the British Library.

ISBN 978-1-898481-74-4

Designed in Scotland by Ian Clydesdale (*www.workhorse.co.uk*)

Printed in China by Hong Kong Graphics & Printing Ltd on rainproof, biodegradable paper

Publisher's note

Individual walkers are responsible for their own welfare and safety, and for being properly equipped for the conditions. The publisher cannot accept liability for any ill-health or injury, however caused, in readers of this book. All information has been checked carefully prior to publication. However, things may change: always follow local signage, and before setting out check this website: *www.cowalway.co.uk*

Feedback is welcome and will be rewarded

All feedback will be followed up, and readers whose comments lead to changes are entitled to claim a free copy of our next edition upon publication. Please email your comments to *info@rucsacs.com*.

9248 8/24 £3

Cowal Way: contents

Foreword

The Cowal Peninsula is a hidden gem which I found by accident when searching for a base for my outdoors business. Everything that the Highlands of Scotland has to offer is here and it is all within an hour or so of the central belt. After years of walking, climbing and trekking the world, I can now do it all from my own doorstep.

Cowal is rich in history, much of it based on its previous inaccessibility. Cut off by the long deep moats of Loch Fyne and Loch Long and hemmed in by the Arrochar mountains in the north, Cowal was settled from the sea. Ferries remain the main means of access, although the Loch Lomond-side road now provides a fast alternative.

The scenery of this hidden gem is typified by the stunning views of the Kyles of Bute, the tranquility of Glendaruel and the spectacular heights of the Arrochar Alps. Add to these the clan histories of the Lamonts, the Campbells and the MacLachlans, together with the many standing stones, burial cairns and rock carvings from the Stone Age and Bronze Age, and Cowal becomes a visitor's paradise.

The Cowal Way was established to connect some of the main heritage sites between the ferry at Portavadie and the road access at Loch Lomond. It is a superb long-distance walk in its own right, and it also links the Kintyre Way to the West Highland Way. The walking varies from the undemanding to the challenging. Completing the Cowal Way produces a sublime and lasting sense of achievement.

James McLuckie

The Cobbler seen from the ruined pier, Loch Long

Planning and preparation

Best time of year

The Cowal peninsula seldom sees extremes of weather and the Cowal Way could in theory be walked at any time of year. However, its latitude (56°North) means that daylight varies from about 18 hours in late June to about six hours in late December. Winter (November to February) is not recommended unless you have a compelling reason. Winter walking must be timed carefully to fit the daylight available, the ground is likely to be sodden and streams are more likely to be in spate.

April, May and June are ideal months, while rhododendrons and wildflowers are at their best, with banks of primroses and bluebells on the lower ground. September and October sometimes offer settled weather, when hills are purple with heather and foliage shows its glorious autumn colours. Cowalfest, the annual outdoor festival, takes place in October, see *www.cowalfest.org*.

July and August are traditionally holiday months, bringing tourists to Cowal and making accommodation scarce. Finding a bed is notoriously difficult during the famous Cowal Highland Gathering (end of August): see *www.cowalgathering. com*. This is also the height of the season for midges (small biting insects that cause maddening itching): *www.midgeforecast.co.uk*

The climate is generally moist. Cowal winters tend to be wet rather than very cold, with snow uncommon but rain and wind likely at any time of year. On high ground especially, the combination of wind and wet can create severe wind chill, so preparation and suitable clothing are essential. Before setting out, check the local weather forecast: see page 70. The weather can change very fast, so always be ready to change your plans.

Terrain and gradients

The Way includes every type of terrain from tidal beach to open moorland. The route links existing rights of way and public footpaths by means of forest tracks and some quiet public roads with a tarmac (sealed) surface.

Elsewhere, the forest roads have loose surfaces, mainly gravel. On public footpaths and certain rights of way, the going is more challenging. Expect some boggy bits unless the weather has been dry for some time. In the upland parts, the route is sometimes narrow, indistinct and steep. Although the difficult stretches are short, they reduce your overall speed to a surprising extent.

The south-west section of the Way is mostly easygoing with gentle gradients and very little altitude gain. Only the Loch Riddon stretch needs some care for the rocky path above the beach among the rhododendrons: see page 35. Timing your walk for low tide avoids some of the difficulties: see page 70 for a web source.

The route is low-level, its highest point, near the cairn shown on page 56, being at a mere 500 m (1640 ft). But don't underestimate the Cowal Way: it offers enormous variety, but at the price of some slow going, especially in the wet. Remember that rough terrain reduces your average speed, and that a group travels at the pace of its slowest member. Overall, you are unlikely to average more than 3 or 4 km/hr (2-2½ mph) unless you are seriously pushing yourselves.

The profile below shows the contrast between the first two low-lying sections and the other three. They rise successively to 360, 350 and 500 m (1180, 1150 and 1640 ft) and only the last section can readily be split (by overnighting at Arrochar).

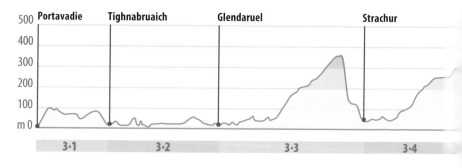

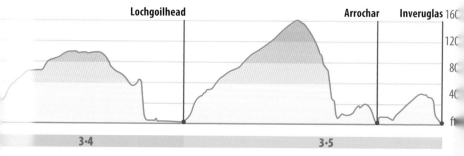

Stepping stones beside Loch Riddon

Previous experience

The Cowal Way is not the ideal choice for your very first long-distance walk, although in fair conditions any healthy person could complete it within five days. But it's never advisable to do your first long hike alone, so seek the company of a more experienced walker. In the sections north of Strachur, if cloud or mist descends, one of you may need to be competent in the use of map and compass.

Whatever your experience, before leaving for Cowal, do several all-day walks, if possible on consecutive days, to test your footwear and to build up fitness. If you will be carrying your belongings for the whole trip, practise hiking with a laden rucksack. Don't under-estimate the longer sections, particularly in energy-sapping, windy or wet conditions. If walking alone or in adverse conditions, always leave a note of your expected arrival time and place. Read page 59 if you intend to climb the Cobbler. For advice on choosing and buying gear, obtain our *Notes for Novices:* see page 71.

Stony path above Lochgoilhead

Days, stages and duration

This guidebook follows the recommended direction, from south-west to north-east. This allows for a gentle start on low-lying terrain, as well as for travel time to Portavadie, which can be reached direct by bus from Dunoon, and which has overnight accommodation. Walking in this direction, the higher, more challenging sections come later, when you are well into your stride.

The final stage from Lochgoilhead to Inveruglas makes a long haul, leading to a late finish at a place with limited accommodation. It can readily be broken by an overnight at Arrochar. You could seize the opportunity to climb the famous Cobbler next day (see page 59), and then complete the walk to Inveruglas. Or, if you're out of time, you can return to Glasgow quickly by walking to Arrochar & Tarbet station (see page 60) or by catching a bus.

The Way begins at Portavadie, where the ferry arrives from Tarbert (Loch Fyne), the northern terminus of the Kintyre Way. It finishes at Inveruglas, where in season a Water Bus ferries people across Loch Lomond to the West Highland Way: see page 70. For ambitious walkers, therefore, the Cowal Way makes a potential link between the southern tip of Kintyre and Fort William at the northern end of the West Highland Way, or even, via the Great Glen Way, all the way to Inverness.

Table 1 presents the Way in five sections, with distances and overnight stops as in the detailed description in Part 3. Many people will follow this linear sequence. Unless you are supported by vehicles with drivers, or can co-ordinate lifts or public transport carefully, you may be carrying a heavy load, or at least your overnight things, spare clothing and a packed lunch. For Cowal Way packages and baggage transfer, visit the website **www.cowalway.co.uk**.

Some will prefer to tackle the Way in sections, which can be completed in any order, as five or six day-walks, or split over a couple of long weekends. If approaching it as day-walks, don't underestimate the driving times to start and finish. Although distances are modest, average speeds can be low, especially on single-track roads where you need to wait in passing places (marked by white diamonds) to pass oncoming traffic and to permit overtaking. In Cowal, all unclassified roads, most B roads and even some A roads are single-track for miles on end.

Table 1
Distances & overnight stops (five-day walk)

	miles	km
Portavadie		
	6·6	10·6
Tighnabruaich		
	11·0	17·7
Glendaruel		
	15·7	25·3
Strachur		
	8·7	14·0
Lochgoilhead		
	15·0	24·1
Inveruglas		
Total	57	92

If walking the Way end-to-end, consider allowing more than five or six walking days for your holiday. This would allow you to split the longer days, to take a break to see local sights, or to have a rest day in bad weather. If time is short, sections 1 and 2 could be combined, but four days is the sensible minimum even for fit walkers. At the other end of the scale, in summer 2015 a cyclist completed the route within a day, despite having to push or carry his bike for about 30% of the time. His blog is linked from our website page **www.rucsacs.com/books/cly**.

Part 4 is about the attractions of the Isle of Bute, which has a long-distance walk of its own, a 13th century castle and other attractions in Rothesay, and the amazing Victorian gothic mansion of Mount Stuart: see pages 64-68. To make Bute a side-trip from the Cowal Way, leave the Way at Glendaruel and use the ferry from Colintraive, allowing an extra night or two for this diversion.

A more radical idea is to set out by ferry from Wemyss Bay to Rothesay, see the sights on Bute and then use its *West Island Way* to reach Rhubodach. From there, it's 5 minutes by ferry to Colintraive, and you can pick up the Cowal Way (to walk in either direction) at Glendaruel. This approach lets you see much more of Bute at the price of walking only part of the Cowal Way.

Whatever your approach to walking the Way, always leave a margin for error. Be aware of tide timings and don't risk running out of daylight. It can be dark by 16.00 in winter.

Pronunciation guide

Cowal place names are mostly pronounced roughly as you might expect, but there are a few puzzling ones. Stress the syllable shown in bold, and try to make the ch sound soft and aspirated. (To get this right, you need to listen to local voices, and try to imitate.)

Allt Robuic	alt rob **ache**
Arrochar	**arr** och ar
Caladh	**cah** la
Colintraive	colin **tryve**
Drimsynie	drim **sine** ie
Dunans	**doo** nans
Glendaruel	glen da **roo** el
Inveruglas	in ver **oo** glus
Portavadie	port a **va** die
Rhubodach	roo **boh** dach
Strachur	strach **urr**
Tighnabruaich	**tine** ah bru ach
(also	**tinn** ah bru ach)

Tarbet versus Tarbert

Distinguish between Tarbet (Loch Lomond), 2 miles east of Arrochar, and Tarbert (Loch Fyne), on Kintyre. Their spelling differs only by an R, but they are 60 miles apart. Both derive from the Gaelic *Tairbeart* meaning a narrow neck of land dividing two lochs; both were used for boat portage by the Vikings.

Accommodation

Table 2: The main facilities along the Cowal Way

	miles from last place	km from last place	B&B/ hotel	campsite	pub/ café	food shop/ carryout
Portavadie			✓		✓	✓
Kames	5·5	8·9	✓		✓	✓
Tighnabruaich	1·1	1·8	✓	✓	✓	✓
Glendaruel (Caravan park)	11·0	17·7	✓	✓		✓
Strachur	15·7	25·3	✓	✓	✓	✓
Lochgoilhead	8·7	14·0	✓		✓	✓
Ardgartan	6·1	9·8	✓			
Arrochar	3·1	5·0	✓		✓	✓
Inveruglas	5·8	9·3			✓	

The sections in Part 3 have been defined by distance, accessibility and likely stopovers for the unsupported walker. Villages along the Way include Tighnabruaich, Glendaruel, Strachur, Lochgoilhead and Arrochar, with shops as well as various accommodation options. Glendaruel has limited options, at or near the Caravan Park, which is over 2 miles north of Clachan of Glendaruel. For details of accommodation and baggage transfer, see **www.cowalway.co.uk**.

Table 1 (on page 8) shows distances for a five-day walk with overnights at the first four villages, but some people will wish to add an extra night at Arrochar with good reason. Cowal's main centre is Dunoon, and you could schedule a night here if arriving from Glasgow by train and ferry from Gourock, reaching Portavadie by bus next day: see page 70.

On arrival at Inveruglas, walkers could return to Arrochar, continue by bus to Ardlui (which has a campsite and other accommodation) or (in season) cross by ferry to Inversnaid on the West Highland Way where there's a hotel and bunkhouse. Tarbet (Loch Lomond) also has accommodation, and (in season) a Water Bus service to Inversnaid: see page 70. The southbound Scottish Citylink bus passes through Inveruglas ('Sloy') and Tarbet *en route* to Glasgow.

The Cowal Way is starting to attract companies that offer a holiday package including accommodation and baggage transfer. They may shuttle walkers to and from each section of walking, which gives more flexibility over accommodation options. If you are planning your holiday with the support of a car and driver, you too can adapt the idea of using lifts back-and-forth each day from a base. Self-catering chalets and cottages are widely

Micro lodge, Glendaruel Caravan park

available in Cowal. Some hotels and B&Bs also offer support services: it's worth asking whether help is available before booking.

Finally, be aware that under the *Scottish Outdoor Access Code*, wild camping is allowed for a couple of nights anywhere that access rights apply, but various responsibilities accompany that right: see the panel on page 16.

Waymarking

Each section of the route is marked by a timber information board at its start and finish. In late 2015, a total of over 150 timber waymarkers with logo were installed along the route. Where parts of the route are shared e.g. with the Three Lochs Way route, the Cowal Way markers may appear alongside other route markers. On the highest, most remote parts of the Way you may also see white posts.

The route can be followed from the Cowal Way waymarkers, backed up by the mapping in this book and the directions in Part 3. However, in adverse conditions you may need the skills to follow compass bearings. North-east of Strachur, especially beyond Lochgoilhead, the route uses open hillside, where visibility may be a problem and waymarkers may not be intervisible.

Tide awareness

The Way starts at sea level and skirts the sea at several locations. Loch Riddon, Loch Fyne, Loch Goil and Loch Long are all sea lochs, long fingers of water extending from the open estuary of the Firth of Clyde. With the latter three, the path is always well clear of the beach and only the scenery is affected by the state of the tide.

On Loch Riddon, however, a walker's progress along the beach can be halted by high tide, making for a delay or perhaps a rocky detour inland. There are normally two high tides each day, about 12½ hours apart. Each day, the high tides fall about one hour later, so a rough guide to each day's tides can be worked out from day one.

Local newspapers, hotels, bars and a tide app on the official website can give you precise tide times, and the website link on page 70 lets you plan ahead.

The narrows at Colintraive

The Way passing along the beach at Loch Riddon

Travel planning

To visitors, Cowal feels like an island. Most people arrive by sea, using one of four ferries. A minority reach Cowal by road, mainly via Glasgow using the A82 trunk road along the west bank of Loch Lomond.

Two ferries operate from the mainland at Gourock, both taking 20-30 minutes. Argyll Ferries operates an hourly service for passengers only from Gourock railway station to Dunoon pier. Western Ferries operate a frequent vehicle service from McInroy's Point, two miles west of Gourock, to Hunter's Quay, 2½ miles north of Dunoon.

A Calmac vehicle ferry plies from Colintraive to the northern tip of Bute, taking about 5 minutes. A longer crossing (about 35 minutes) links Wemyss Bay on the mainland (30 miles west of Glasgow) with Rothesay, Bute's main centre. The Calmac ferry from Tarbert Loch Fyne (on Kintyre) to Portavadie takes 30 minutes.

All of the Cowal vehicle ferries are ro-ro (roll-on, roll-off) and bookings are not needed or taken. At very busy periods a ferry may be full, entailing a wait of up to an hour for the next one.

Arriving by train, the nearest mainline stations are in Glasgow. From England and the south and west, trains arrive at Central Station, which is also the terminal for onward travel to Cowal. Trains connect with the Argyll ferry from Gourock after a journey of about 45 minutes. Trains from the east and north of Scotland arrive at Queen Street station and passengers must transfer to Glasgow Central for Cowal connections.

To reach (or return from) the northern end of the Cowal Way, take the Fort William train which connects Glasgow Queen Street with Arrochar (journey time about 1¼ hours). However, check times carefully as the service is limited. The bus service is more frequent, cheaper and quicker: see page 70.

Arriving by air, from Glasgow Airport transfer to Paisley Gilmour Street station and take the train to Gourock. Trains from Prestwick Airport also stop at Gilmour Street. Contacts for ferry and train timetables are on page 70.

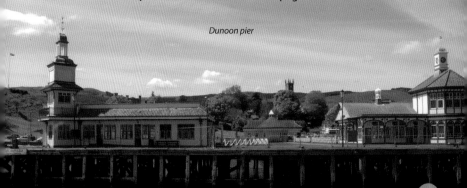

Dunoon pier

Bus travel

Glasgow's bus station is at Buchanan Street, next to Queen Street rail station, with a wide range of buses to Cowal, Kintyre and Argyll. Scottish Citylink's 901/906 service reaches the ferry terminal at Gourock (for Dunoon) in just over an hour. Table 3 shows distances from various places to Gourock, which is about 25 miles west of Glasgow.

Its Fort William route (914/915/916) stops at Tarbet (Loch Lomond) and Inveruglas (ask for *Sloy*) with a journey time of about an hour. Scottish Citylink's 926 service to Campbeltown in Kintyre goes via Tarbert Loch Fyne, but the 107-mile journey takes over 3 hours to reach Tarbert, and you still need a ferry to reach Portavadie. If travelling by car, however, you could consider parking at Tarbet and then taking the bus to Tarbert to start your walk.

Table 3 Distances to Gourock for Dunoon Ferry	miles	km
Glasgow city centre	28	45
Glasgow Airport	20	32
Edinburgh Airport	67	107
Prestwick Airport	42	67
London	439	690

Within Cowal, each of the villages along the Way is connected to Dunoon by a West Coast Motors service. Dunoon to Portavadie buses (478/479) run at least twice a day and take just over an hour, but the timetable varies, depending on school holidays. Contacts for timetables are given on page 70.

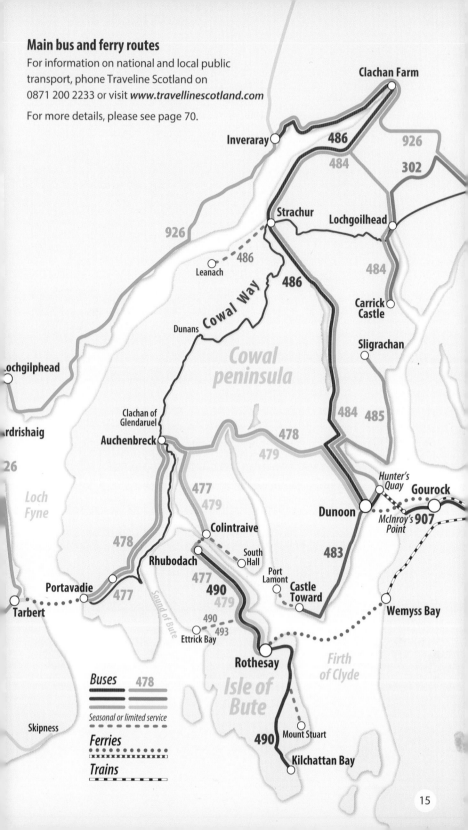

Main bus and ferry routes

For information on national and local public transport, phone Traveline Scotland on 0871 200 2233 or visit *www.travellinescotland.com*

For more details, please see page 70.

Clachan Farm

Inveraray

486

926

484

302

Strachur

Lochgoilhead

926

486

Leanach

Cowal Way

486

Dunans

Carrick Castle

484

Cowal peninsula

Sligrachan

ochgilphead

Clachan of Glendaruel

Auchenbreck

484 485

478

479

rdrishaig

26

Loch Fyne

477
479

478

Hunter's Quay

Gourock

Dunoon

McInroy's Point

907

Colintraive

South Hall

483

Rhubodach

Port Lamont

Castle Toward

477

477

490

479

Portavadie

478

490
493

Wemyss Bay

Tarbert

Ettrick Bay

Sound of Bute

Rothesay

Firth of Clyde

Isle of Bute

Buses 478

Skipness

Seasonal or limited service

Ferries

Mount Stuart

490

Kilchattan Bay

Trains

Dogs

Responsible owners are entitled to take their dogs along the Way. However, think carefully before deciding to bring your pet. Dogs must be kept under close control, not only to avoid stress to livestock and wildlife, but also for their own safety. If you are walking with your dog on the lead, keep well away from cattle: both dog and owner are endangered by this combination. Before deciding to take your dog along the Way, consider these points:

1 Some sections of the Way have stiles that you will have to lift your dog over. This can be strenuous and/or awkward, depending on the dog's weight and attitude.

2 Many accommodations do not accept dogs: check carefully before booking.

3 If your dog fouls the path, please clear up after it.

4 Dogs may disturb ground-nesting birds or young mammals: keep your dog under extra-close control during the breeding season (April to June).

Everyone has the right to be on most land and inland water providing they act responsibly. Your access rights and responsibilities are explained fully in the Scottish Outdoor Access Code.

KNOW THE CODE BEFORE YOU GO
outdooraccess-scotland.com

Whether you're in the outdoors or managing the outdoors, the key things are to
• **take responsibility for your own actions** • **respect the interests of other people** • **care for the environment.**
Find out more by visiting *www.outdooraccess-scotland.com* or by contacting Scottish Natural Heritage; see page 70 for details.

Your rights and responsibilities when walking with a dog are explained in the leaflet *Dog Owners* from Scottish Natural Heritage: see page 69.
The *Scottish Outdoor Access Code* interprets access rights established by law: see the panel above. The Cowal Way passes through countryside which provides a livelihood for its residents. It is your responsibility to show consideration for them and their livestock.

Lambing takes places between March and June: never disturb pregnant ewes, nor approach young lambs. Cattle can be fiercely protective of their young. Give them a wide berth, especially if calves are around.

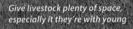

Give livestock plenty of space, especially it they're with young

Packing checklist

This list separates essential and desirable items. If you haven't worn your waterproof trousers recently, test them before you go, while there's still time to re-proof, mend or replace them. Gaiters are great for keeping boots and feet dry and mud-free, and for protection from brambles, nettles and bracken where ticks may lurk. Take hat and sunscreen for sun protection. Walking poles may be useful for balance on boggy ground, when stream crossing and on the steeper gradients.

If you are camping, you will need much more gear (tent, sleeping bag and mat, food and cooking kit) and a much larger rucksack in which to carry everything. If wild camping, remember that water should be boiled or purified before drinking.

Essential

- rucksack with waterproof cover or liner(s)
- comfortable, waterproof walking boots
- specialist walking socks
- waterproof jacket and over-trousers
- clothing in layers (tops, trousers, jacket)
- hat (for warmth and/or sun protection)
- gloves
- guidebook, maps and compass
- whistle and torch (for emergencies)
- water carrier and plenty of water (or purification tablets)
- enough food to last between supply points
- first aid kit, including blister treatment
- toilet tissue (preferably biodegradable)
- personal toiletries
- insect repellent and sun protection
- cash and credit cards (there are few cash machines); phone boxes may take only cash (40p minimum) or only cards.

Desirable

- walking poles
- gaiters
- trainers, especially for road-walking
- spare dry socks to change into
- camera with plenty of spare memory or film
- spare camera batteries
- binoculars – useful for watching wildlife
- notebook and pen
- pouch or secure pockets for keeping small items handy and safe
- mobile phone.

 Mobile phone reception is very patchy in Cowal. Never rely on one for personal safety. In 2016, the network with best coverage was Vodafone. There are few working public telephones, but in a real emergency a local resident may help you out.

2·1 The Cowal peninsula

Geography

The Cowal peninsula lies about 30 miles (50 km) west of Glasgow, surrounded by sea and hills. Geographically it lies in the south-west of the Scottish Highlands, whilst administratively it falls under Argyll & Bute Council. Paradoxically, it is both very accessible and almost unknown. It has much to recommend it: natural beauty, deep peace and wilderness, and a long, fascinating history.

The origin of the name *Cowal* is disputed. It may derive from *Comhgall*, a 6th century prince of the Gaels, or may come from an ancient Norse word meaning 'fork of land'. To the south, the land certainly divides into three 'prongs': two of these, shaped like a lobster claw, almost enclose the Isle of Bute, separated by narrows called the Kyles (*straits*) of Bute. The peninsula is defined by Loch Fyne to its west and Loch Long and the Firth of Clyde to its east. To the north, it is bounded by the belt of mountains between the heads of Loch Fyne and Loch Long.

Inland the terrain is hilly and divided by deep glens with many hill tops in the north exceeding 2000 ft (610 m). Apart from the extreme south-west (Ardlamont) and around Dunoon, most of Cowal lies above 650 ft (200 m) except for the glen floors and narrow, rocky coastal strips.

The peninsula is about 30 miles long and up to 15 miles (25 km) wide. Access by road is mainly via the A82 trunk road from Glasgow and the A83, over the *Rest and Be Thankful* pass. Bus and ferry connections are shown on page 15.

The population of Cowal is fewer than 20,000, most of whom live in or around Dunoon, Cowal's effective 'capital'. The Way passes instead through Cowal's villages: Tighnabruaich, Glendaruel, Strachur, Lochgoilhead and Arrochar. Services, including public transport, are limited and visitors should take nothing for granted.

Burnt Islands, Kyles of Bute

Looking down the East Kyle from Colintraive

Cowal shares the mild, moist climate typical of the western Highlands, with extremes of temperature uncommon. The prevailing wind is from the Atlantic, and annual rainfall is 80 inches (2000 mm), compared with Glasgow which has about half that amount. This benign damp climate allows palm trees and sub-tropical plants to flourish in roadside gardens. Hot summer days can be idyllic with glorious blue skies, deserted beaches and seemingly endless evenings.

Glendaruel, a flat-bottomed valley formed by a glacier

Geology

The Cowal peninsula lies to the north of the Highland Boundary Fault, a geological feature which cuts across mainland Scotland from south-west to north-east, crossing the southern part of Loch Lomond, clipping the south-east tip of Cowal and dividing the Isle of Bute. So all of Cowal and the northern part of Bute are in the Highlands.

The fault separates two distinct geological regions. To the north and west lie hard metamorphic rocks of the Cambrian and Pre-cambrian periods. These are marine deposits which have been changed by intense pressure and temperature into schists, slates and other rocks, predominantly grey but often with white quartz veins. To the south and east are Old Red Sandstone conglomerates, softer sedimentary rocks of the Devonian and Carboniferous periods. The lowland sandstones have a toehold only at Cowal's south-eastern tip.

The change in scenery between south and north Cowal reflects underlying geology – from fertile low-lying fields and farmland to the bare craggy mountains just 25 miles to the north. The landscape is also a visible record of past climate change. The ice ages, the last of which ended only 10,000 years ago, left their marks everywhere.

Glacial erosion scoured out the main glens, forming U-shaped, steep-sided valleys. Most of the long narrow lochs were formed when valleys drowned after the ice melted. After the retreat of massive, heavy glaciers, the land was released from intense pressure and rose in level, resulting in many raised beaches throughout the area.

Look out for isolated huge boulders (glacial 'erratics') which were transported and deposited by the glaciers. The boulder photographed below is on the Way above Lochgoilhead: see page 56.

2·2 History and heritage

Over the last six thousand years, Stone Age and Bronze Age people left enduring marks on Cowal in the form of their burial cairns, rock carvings and hut traces. Standing stones and cup marks anywhere from 2500 to 6000 years old are still mysterious and controversial, but they certainly indicate a settled population. South-west Cowal seems to have been quite densely populated. Finds of post holes, pottery and flint tools in Glendaruel suggest the existence of 5000-year old huts.

By 800 AD the Norse invasion had started and at the height of their power the Vikings controlled most of the north of Scotland and all of the western isles. However, Argyll was never completely subdued and it underwent a period of upheaval lasting nearly 500 years.

In 1093 Malcolm King of Scots made a treaty with Magnus King of Norway which gave the latter 'all the islands off the west coast separated by water navigable by a ship with the rudder set'. Magnus, in order to claim the whole Kintyre peninsula, promptly had his galley dragged on rollers for nearly a mile across the isthmus at Tarbert: see photograph below. The Vikings raided, but they also settled, leaving a legacy of Norse names such as Loch Long, named after the longships, and Ormidale, valley of the snakes.

Medieval times in Cowal were turbulent, with endless disputes, battles and marriages between the emerging clans. The Way starts in traditional Clan Lamont country at Portavadie and crosses through Campbell and MacLachlan country to reach MacFarlane lands near Loch Sloy in the north. Castles such as the Lamont ruins at Asgog and Toward were built as strongholds, abandoned only after they were destroyed by Campbell sieges: see panel.

Asgog Castle

This ivy-covered, ruinous tower house was built in the mid-15th century by a junior branch of the Lamont clan, to fortify their hold on south-west Cowal. In 1646 the Campbells besieged the royalist Lamonts, both at Asgog and at Toward Castle, south of Dunoon. Finally, on receiving guarantees of safety, the Lamont clan chief ordered the defenders of both castles to surrender. The Campbells ignored their promises, instead sacking and burning the castles. Many of the defenders were killed or buried alive, and 36 leading Lamonts were taken to Dunoon to be hanged in public.

Aerial view of Tarbert, Loch Fyne

Asgog Castle

The clan system operated whenever there was a national call to arms, as in the Jacobite rebellions of 1715 and 1745. After the Battle of Culloden (1746) marked the end of clan autonomy, the London-based government outlawed weapons, the wearing of tartan and the playing of pipes. The MacLachlan castle near Strachur was destroyed in reprisal for the clan's support of Bonnie Prince Charlie.

To establish control of the Highlands, General Wade set up permanent garrisons of soldiers throughout Scotland and built good roads to link them. The military road over the spectacular *Rest and Be Thankful* pass between Loch Lomondside and Inveraray was built in 1748 by Wade's successor Major Caulfeild. The modern A83 clings to the hillside, but the old road is easily seen to its left, running along the floor of Glen Croe, finally climbing very steeply to the pass.

In 1775 one of the first roads to be linked to the military system under the government's Great Roads Act was built to connect Ardlamont in the south with Loch Fyne, in effect creating a precursor to the Cowal Way.

Up to then, little had changed in the way of life of the Cowal population since the arrival of the Norsemen. Subsistence farming was the norm, with cattle and goats kept for meat, leather and dairy produce. Peat was used for fuel, conserving precious wood for use in building and making charcoal. Families lived in small settlements of a few houses near a source of water. Many of these abandoned settlements can still be seen, often with only a gable wall left standing.

At the other end of the social scale were the lairds' houses. During a prosperous period in the nineteenth century, these became grander. Ardlamont, Ormidale, Castle Lachlan, Dunans and Strachur House are still occupied. Victorian 'castles' were created or extended from earlier buildings at places such as Benmore, Caladh Harbour, Drimsynie and Glendaruel. Sadly, Caladh Castle (see page 35) was destroyed after World War 2 and Glendaruel House burned down in 1970. However, its historic main gate is still a feature of the Way: see page 40.

Dunoon, Tighnabruaich and Lochgoilhead expanded and prospered in Victorian times with the building of grand villas for the 'merchant princes'. These were successful businessmen who chose to live in rural splendour and commute daily to work in Glasgow. Their journeys were made possible by fast steamer connections. Leaving their seaside mansions early, they breakfasted aboard the steamer and would arrive fresh in their Glasgow offices after a shorter journey time than is possible by car today.

Steamers also brought tourists deep into Cowal via Loch Riddon, Loch Fyne, Loch Long and even Loch Lomond. The beautiful Kyles of Bute and the rugged heights of the Arrochar Alps could be enjoyed from the deck of steamers and from coaches. Ferry tours offered circular routes from Glasgow, taking in the whole peninsula. Cowal had arrived as a tourist destination.

The Waverley paddle-steamer at Blairmore Pier

2·3 Habitats and wildlife

Cowal's underlying geology determines the various habitats encountered on the Way from south-west to north-east:

• coastal • river valley and farmland • woodland • moor and upland.

Coastal

The south-west part of the Way is mainly at or near sea level, and the Way returns to sea level again at Strachur, Lochgoilhead and Arrochar. Indeed, nowhere in Argyll Forest Park is more than 5 miles (8 km) from salt water. Common and grey seals may be seen, watching inquisitively. Grey seals have more pointed heads than common, and a heavier body shape. Common (or harbour) seals

Eider duck (male)

have more mottled coats, and often arch their slimmer bodies when basking on rocks. Their nostrils form a distinctive V-shape when seen from the front.

Sea birds are plentiful, notably red-breasted merganser and eider duck, the latter easily recognised by its distinctive 'ah-ooo' call. Equally distinctive is the oystercatcher, a striking bird with black and white plumage and a long orange bill. These birds often feed in flocks on the beach. When disturbed, their piercing shrieks and the M-shaped pattern on their wings in flight are unmistakable.

Male grey seal (Halichoerus grypus)

Other common seabirds include gulls, fulmars and gannets. Cormorants and their smaller cousins, shags, are often to be seen on rocks, drying out their wings in the sun. Gannets are easily recognisable by their behaviour, gliding over the water in search of fish, then climbing and dive-bombing steeply to make their catch.

Of particular interest is the Ruel estuary, where you can see the transition from marine to river ecosystem. There's a heronry beside Loch Riddon, where otters may also be sighted. In the same quiet river pool, just touched by the effects of a high tide, we have seen both otter and seal hunting for salmon – albeit not at the same time.

Grey heron nesting, with chicks

Otter feeding on codling

Barn owl in hawthorn tree

River valley and farmland

Cowal's rivers are mostly short in length and very variable in volume – feeble in dry weather but foaming torrents when in spate after heavy rain. These are ideal conditions for salmon and sea trout, and several of the larger rivers are well known for sport fishing. Glendaruel on the other hand is a classic glaciated valley. As the ice melted at the end of the last Ice Age, the glen was flooded, firstly from the sea. River silting gradually built up the flood plain, creating flat farmland very different from the hills on either side.

The rivers and streams, with their many pools, waterfalls and gorges, provide ideal conditions for native broadleaves, where sheep and deer can't easily destroy them. Bluebells and primroses are also common here on road verges, adding welcome colour to the tarmac stretches of the Way.

Fields, meadows and verges are home to the delightful barn owl, which preys on mice, voles and rats. It is one of the few owls that can be spotted in daytime, especially at dawn and dusk. Although the barn owl is widely distributed worldwide (being found, like the osprey, on every continent except Antarctica) their population has been declining. This is mainly because intensive agricultural practice drives out their prey, but Cowal is a good place to see this rare bird. They nest in traditional sites, using trees as well as undisturbed farm buildings and outhouses.

Lephinkill Farm, Glendaruel

Woodland

Argyll Forest Park dates from 1935 and was Britain's first, set up both to grow timber and provide for public recreation. Although productive conifers dominate its scenery – with over 70% sitka spruce – Cowal is also home to a wide variety of trees.

The Way passes through several areas of mixed woodland with oak, beech, ash and rowan, and also Scots pine. The broadleaf woodland at Portavadie is a nature reserve, with good specimens of north atlantic oak (*quercus petraea*). It is home to rare nightjars and natterer bats (*myotis natteri*), as well as common woodland animals such as fox and red squirrel.

Roe deer (doe)

Roe deer also prefer the thicker cover of woodland to the open hillside. Smaller than their red cousins, they travel alone or in small family groups, with hind and fawn often very close. If you walk quietly, you may surprise them, and see their pale rumps bouncing as they flee for cover.

Cowal's climate, similar to that of west coast America, proved irresistible to the Victorian tree planters. Look out for specimen trees in the grounds of the 'big houses'. Many Douglas Fir and Wellingtonia are over 150 years old and some are more than 200 ft (60 m) high. The Way borders the Lochgoilhead Arboretum, which boasts several specimens on the Tree Register of the British Isles.

In spring, native woodland is home to wild flowers such as wood anemone, wood sorrel, wild garlic, primrose and violet. Rhododendrons and azaleas abound, with their bright colours adding to those of the heather and gorse. The Lauder walks at Glenbranter are excellent for bluebells.

Fox in woodland

Cowal, like Arran and Kintyre, is one of the last strongholds of the red squirrel. In autumn these delightful creatures collect food and nesting material for winter storage. The non-native grey squirrel is present around Lochs Long and Lomond and threatens the red population, because greys carry the squirrelpox virus that is fatal to reds. Grey squirrels also compete strongly for food, each one weighing twice as much as its slender red cousin. So far,

Red squirrel

local efforts to repel the greys seem to be succeeding, but protecting the vulnerable red squirrel population of Cowal is a conservation priority. To report squirrel sightings (red or grey), visit ***www.scottishsquirrels.org.uk***.

Moor and upland

The northern sections of the walk from Strachur to Arrochar climb steeply through moorland toward mountain, with a high point of 500 m (1640 ft) above Lochgoilhead. Vegetation changes along the way, with bracken, conifers and gorse giving way to rough grass.

Above the tree line is open hillside and crag, terrain favoured by the golden eagle – iconic bird of the Highlands. It needs a huge hunting area, and Cowal supports only 3-4 pairs: keep a look-out over high ground. The wings are long and rectangular, with a span of 5-8 feet (1·5-2·4 m), held straight when soaring, or flapped with a very slow wingbeat. Typically seen from a great distance, their size can be hard to judge, but their proportions are distinctive.

Buzzard are much more common, particularly below the tree line. Also known as the 'tourist's eagle', they have a smaller wing span – about 4-5 feet (1·2-1·5 m). Their heads look larger in proportion, and the wings make a shallow V-shape when soaring. Buzzards' mewing call is also distinctive. Often they compete with crows for carrion, not always successfully.

Buzzard feeding on rabbit

Black and red grouse also live on moorland, but are more often heard then seen. They were a factor in the local decision-making process for siting the Cruach Mhor wind farm. The local black grouse population had to be encouraged to move further along the ridge before the project could go ahead.

Red grouse

The open hill is also the domain of red deer, which graze in small herds on the high ridges. Spiralling population growth has led to culling, to prevent death by slow starvation. Deer feed on young conifer needles and the bark of some trees such as willow and rowan. Telltale signs include torn bark and broken stems where new growth has been nibbled. Scarred trees show where they've scraped the velvet off growing antlers, and black peaty wallows mark where they like to roll.

The beauty of Cowal is that all of these habitats and their associated wildlife can be enjoyed in a single visit. Beaches are overlooked by high mountains and it's possible to see seal, red squirrel, deer and perhaps even eagle in the course of a single day's walk.

Red deer stag in rut

29

Distance	6·6 miles 10·6 km
Terrain	mostly track or path, with stretches of open ground and gorse, final 3 km on quiet roads
Grade	gentle climb to 85 m (280 ft) over the first 2 km, then on easily undulating track
Food and drink	Portavadie marina (restaurant, café, shops), Kames and Tighnabruaich (accommodation, cafés, shops)
Summary	undemanding section with fine views back over Loch Fyne to Kintyre, and over and alongside the Kyles of Bute

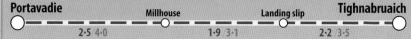

Portavadie   Millhouse   Landing slip   Tighnabruaich

2·5 / 4·0   1·9 / 3·1   2·2 / 3·5

- From Portavadie ferry terminal, head east along the concrete road and continue uphill past the marina for 250 m. Turn left at the forest road signed for Asgog.

- Continue for 700 m to where the road turns sharply left, by an overhead power line. Turn right on to a grassy path with another sign to Asgog and a marker post. Follow the path for 100 m through bracken to a clearing with houses and ruins.

- Follow the marker on the right of the clearing and continue uphill to the left of the tree line. After 200 m the path steepens, swinging right up to a high point at about 85 m above sea level.

Portavadie ferry leaving for Tarbert

- The Way then descends for 250 m across cleared forest, before bearing left to go steeply downhill, across a gully.

- Join the forest road for a few hundred metres before turning right by a standing stone, along a trod path. The path continues above the ruins of Asgog Castle before swinging right and descending to the shore.

- Turn left and follow the path to the gate at the top of the loch. Pass through the gate or over the stile and follow the shoreline.

- Near the head of the loch, there are cottages. Go uphill diagonally across the field for 150 m to a gatepost on the skyline. Follow the farm road downhill for 300 m to meet the B8000.

- Turn right and continue for 300 m to the Millhouse crossroads. Turn left on to the Kames road, noticing the ruins of the powder mill buildings to your right: see panel.

- After 500 m, next to Cladh a Mhuillinn Lodge, note the small roadside cannon and bell post: see photo above.

i

Powder Mill

Gunpowder manufacture began in Millhouse in 1839, helped by the readily available water power and charcoal. Despite various accidents, it continued until 1921, and the ruins are still visible in the woods to the right of the Kames road. Safety features included the separation of the buildings, trees to baffle any blast and massive walls.

The small cannon in the photograph was a powder tester, designed to fire a standard ball a certain distance if the powder was right. The rusted ball stuck in its barrel confirms the unpredictable nature of the activity.

- Cross the stile into the field just beyond the Lodge entrance. Cross uphill to the gated stile and into the next field, keeping the same heading.

- The path rises through thick gorse for 300 m before passing on to open ground. Cross a second gate-stile.

- Through the gate, continue ahead to a golf fairway. Just before the golfing green, cross the ditch by timber sleepers and then cross the fairway, making sure that no golf balls are in play.

- A track leads from the fairway past the end of a forest, revealing your first views of the Kyles of Bute. Follow it downhill under the power lines. Bear right at the golf course road, and, after 200 m, swing back below the power lines again.

- Within 60 m, take the narrow path on the left that descends 1 km to the shore at Kames. This is the historic 'green road' used to transport gunpowder by horse and cart, turfed to avoid the horses' shoes striking sparks off the stones.

- Descend to the car park, noticing the World War II tank landing slip at its far end. Turn sharp left along the shore road for 1·3 km to the Kames Hotel, where the road zigzags uphill and passes behind it.

- Turn right past the Kyles Church and public toilets to a crossroads with shop and bus stop. Turn right along the B8000 for 1·5 km to reach Tighnabruaich.

The Kames Hotel

Tighnabruaich seen from Kames

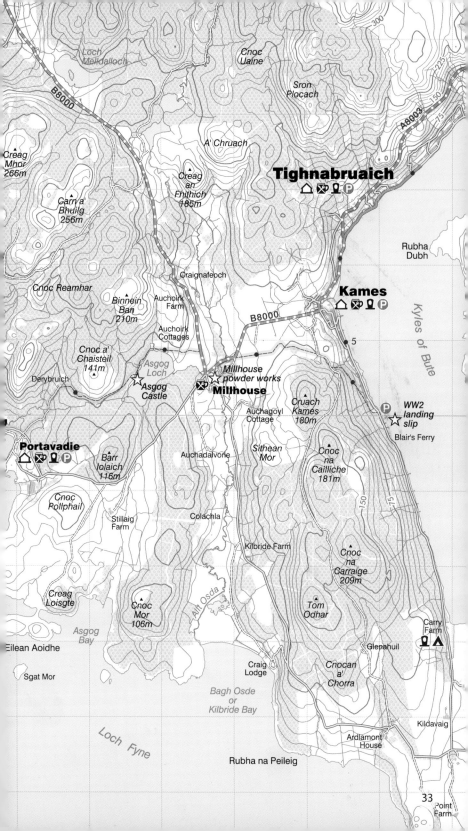

Loch Melldalloch

B8000

Cnoc Uaine

Sron Plocach

300

A'Chruach

A8003

225
150
75

Creag Mhor 266m

Creag an Fhithich 185m

Tighnabruaich

Rubha Dubh

Carn a' Bhuilg 256m

Cnoc Reamhar

Craignafeoch

Kames

Binnein Ban 210m

Auchoirk Farm

B8000

5

Kyles of Bute

Auchoirk Cottages

Cnoc a' Chaisteil 141m

Asgog Loch

Millhouse powder works

Derybruich

Asgog Castle

Millhouse

Auchagoyl Cottage

Cruach Kames 180m

WW2 landing slip

Blair's Ferry

Portavadie

Barr Iolaich 116m

Auchadalvorie

Sithean Mor

Cnoc na Cailliche 181m

150

75

Cnoc Rollphail

Stillaig Farm

Colachla

Kilbride Farm

Cnoc na Carraige 209m

Creag Loisgte

Asgog Bay

Eilean Aoidhe

Sgat Mor

Cnoc Mor 106m

Allt Osda

Tom Odhar

Carry Farm

Glenahuil

Craig Lodge

Cnocan a' Chorra

Kildavaig

Bagh Osde or Kilbride Bay

Loch Fyne

Ardlamont House

Rubha na Peileig

33

Point Farm

Tighnabruaich

Tighnabruaich is one of the largest villages in Cowal, and by road it sits 'at the end of the line'. Perched on the Kyles (the narrows between Cowal and Bute), it is probably still more accessible by sea than by road.

Tighnabruaich means 'house on the hill'. Seen from the water, its houses stretch up the steep mountain-side from directly behind the sea wall. The 'new road' from Glendaruel – 'the finest short drive in Scotland' – was completed only in 1969. Until then, the tortuous road down Loch Fyne-side provided the only access.

Once just a fishing village on a sheltered bay, it really flourished with the coming of the steamships. The many fine houses along the sea front were built by wealthy Glasgow merchants. Look out for delicate examples of ironwork, stained glass windows and exotic gardens as you walk through.

With three piers, all built in Victorian times, the village could handle up to a hundred boats a day, many of them steamers carrying tourists. In its heyday, a trip 'doon the watter' was a great day out from Glasgow. Tighnabruaich Pier, one of the few surviving working wooden piers on the Firth of Clyde, is now a Listed Building.

Other frequent callers at the piers were the Clyde puffers – small cargo boats which delivered vital supplies around the west coast. They had flat bottoms to let them beach and unload at low tide, essential to supply remote settlements without suitable piers. Typical cargoes included coal and furniture, with farm produce and gravel sometimes being brought back

During World War 2, Tighnabruaich's sheltered waters proved ideal for Combined Operations Training. A training camp, HMS James Cook, was set up at Caladh in 1942 for landing craft operations. The Way passes its concrete tank landing slip at Kames.

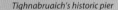

Tighnabruaich's historic pier

3·2 Tighnabruaich to Glendaruel

Distance	**11·0 miles 17·7 km**
Terrain	**mostly tracks and roads, with 1·5 km of woodland path**
Grade	**mainly low-lying, but with a stiff climb to 50 m, followed by 1·5 km of more challenging woodland route**
Food and drink	**Tighnabruaich (hotel, shops), Glendaruel (caravan park shop, in season)**
Summary	**mainly easy walking along pavement and private road alongside the Kyles of Bute, later on 9 km of quiet road through Glendaruel, with a short, challenging stretch in between**

Tighnabruaich ●━━━━━━━━━━○ **Ormidale Lodge** ━━━━━━━━━━○ **Clachan** ━━○ **Glendaruel** ●
 4·4/7·1   4·6 /7·4   2·0 /3·2

- From Tighnabruaich village centre, follow the shore road alongside the Kyles of Bute for 1·6 km. Look back for views of Arran's mountains, beyond the Kyles.

- After the houses and tarmac give out, follow the track through the boatyard, then continue along the the Caladh Estate private road, reaching a fork after 1 km.

- Bear left uphill through the woods to a bridge and waterfall. After 150 m, the track swings left to a junction where you keep straight ahead, descending to the shoreline.

- Continue for 550 m to the head of a small bay and a further 120 m to pass the idyllic Caladh harbour, nestling between shore and Eilean Dubh on your right. On the left are the rubble remains of Caladh Castle, a Victorian mansion requisitioned by the navy and blown up after World War 2.

- The track bends left and then right and after 100 m reaches a crossways where, if you divert a few steps up to the left, you'll find an information board about Caladh Castle.

- At the crossways go straight ahead through woodland, following the road as it undulates and descends to shore level.

- After a further 550 m, pass between metal boat sheds. Take the path on your right, just before two white houses, down to the shore.

- Turn left and follow the shoreline north to the corner of the last field. Expect slow progress for the next 1·5 km to Ormidale Lodge, although major improvements were made to this section in 2015. The revised route, including steps and boardwalk, offers some great views.

- Take the waymarked trod path through the trees above the beach for 500 m to reach a group of massive fallen boulders, or at low tide simply walk along the beach.

- Pass the boulders on the beach or go through a narrow passage among them. A third option is a rocky scramble above the boulders. Your choice will depend on the state of the tide: see page 70 for a website with tide tables.

Falls near Upper Caladh

Lephinkill

Creag na Sgeith

15

Bealachandrain

Waulkmill

Kandahar Cottage

Coille Mhor

A886

Cruach nan Tarbh 349m

An Cnap

A8003

Fasgadh Stronafian

B836

Ormidale

River Ruel

Auchenbreck

Cruach Camuilt 345m

Lochhead Cottage South

Ardachuple Lodge

Meckan's Grave ☆

Cruach nan Caorach 458m

Cruach nam Broighleag 415m

Shellfield

Ardachuple Farm

Heronry ☆

Craig Cottage

Loch Riddon (Ruel)

Ormidale Lodge

Tigh-Na-Cedaraich

Creagan Dubh

Kinlochruel

Beinn Bhreac 454m

Fearnoch

Glen Caladh Farm

10

B866

Binnein Mor

300

The Birches

Caladh Harbour ☆

Beinn Capuill 438m

225

Eilean Dubh

Kyles of Bute

Eilean Mor

A886

Colintraive

West Glen Cottage

15

Rhubodach

Rhubodach Cottage

Rubha Bhain

A8003

Isle of Bute

Tighnabruaich

37

- Just beyond the boulders, take the trod path to the left, rising among the rhododendrons. Follow the path as it winds and climbs through the woods.

- The rocky path runs for 500 m to Ormidale Lodge (Craig Lodge), rising to 50 m above sea level.

- Descend from behind Ormidale Lodge and emerge (with care) on to the public road. Turn left to follow the road for 2 km, passing a heronry on a small headland to your right, to the junction with the A8003 by Shellfield Farm.

- Turn right and follow the single-track A8003 for 3·5 km. Just before the bridge over the River Ruel, turn left on to a side road that passes Waulkmill Cottage. The road beyond runs for 600 m to a footbridge over the Bealachandrain Burn.

Walkway and viewpoint near Ormidale Lodge

- Cross the bridge and turn right on to the tarmac road. Follow the road for 150 m before crossing the historic two-arched Telford Bridge (1818) over the Ruel.

- Turn left and continue for 350 m to the junction with the A866 at Lephinkill Farm. Turn left for 300 m and take the junction signposted 'Kilmodan Carved Stones and Clachan of Glendaruel'.

Right: Stone 6, the finest example of the Loch Awe school of carving

Below: Kilmodan Church

Creag
na
Sgeith

Dunans

Creachan
Dubh
470m

Kilbridemore

☆ Dunans
Castle

Strondavor

Garvie Farm

Cailleach a'
Bheathrach

Creachan
Mor

● 20

Conchra

An Cruachan
294m

☆ Kildalvan
ruins

Olacheranmor

Duiletter

wind
farm

Water Mill

Ardacheranmor

Cruach
Mhor
319m

Glendaruel
Caravan
Park

Lucknow
Gates ☆

Ardachearanbeg

Cnocan
Sgeir'e
299m

Cruach
nan
Cullean
432m

Camquhart

Auchategan

ver Camquhart

Clachan of
Glendaruel

Cruach
nam
Mult
279m

An t-Suil
297m

A' Chruach
365m

P

Kilmodan
Church ☆

Lephinkill

15

Creag
na
Sgeith

ealachandrain

Waulkmill

Kandahar Cottage

Coille Mhor

An
Cnap

A886

Fasgadh Stronafian

A8003

B836

River Ruel

39

Ormidale

- Continue for 350 m, passing the former Glendaruel Hotel on your left. Beside the hotel is a small lane to the left leading to Kilmodan Church and its carved stones: see panel.

- After another 150 m take the left fork signed 'Home Farm Cottages' (West Glendaruel Road) and descend for 200 m to a fine stone bridge.

- Cross the Ruel and continue across its flat flood plain. Follow the road for 1 km to Camquhart Farm. Beyond the farm the road passes some roadside crags – remnants of a raised beach.

- Continue for a further 1 km to Maymore Farm. About 200 m beyond, at a fork in the road, stand the Lucknow Gates, formerly the main gates to Glendaruel House, and said to commemorate the 1857 Siege of Lucknow, India.

- Keep left to reach The Water Mill (B&B) (on the left) or Glendaruel Caravan and Camping Park (through a gate on the right.

Kilmodan Church

This historic T-plan church was built in 1783 on the site of earlier churches, perhaps of the 10th or 12th centuries, the most recent dating from 1610. St Modan was an early Celtic saint, contemporary with St Columba (6th century).

The latest church was built with three separate entrances, each with its own gallery. According to legend, the three local Campbell families, Glendaruel, Ormidale and South Hall (Colintraive), each used separate entrances so that they could speak to God without having to speak to each other. The graveyard houses a small building with carved stones (Loch Awe school, from the 14th and 15th centuries). Like the church, this building is unlocked.

Clachan of Glendaruel

Lucknow Gates

3·3 Glendaruel to Strachur

Distance	15·7 miles 25·3 km
Terrain	mainly farm and forest tracks, with final 4 km on quiet road
Grade	starts on low-lying road, then steady climb to 360 m (1180 ft) on forest road and descent almost to sea level
Food and drink	Glendaruel (caravan park shop, in season), Strachur (hotel, pub, tearoom, shops)
Side-trip	Kildalvan (ruined village), Dunans Castle Heritage Trail
Summary	after 7 km of quiet road, a long section of forest road with good views, followed by a gorge with fine falls

Glendaruel　　　　**Garvie Farm**　　　　　　**Allt Robuic gorge**　　**Strachur**

○━━━━━━○━━━━━━━━━━━━━━━━━○━━━━━○

4·2/6·8　　　　　　7·6/12·2　　　　　3·9/6·3

- Continue north on the West Glendaruel Road, or from here take the Home Farm Woodland Walk to your left, which climbs beside attractive waterfalls and rejoins the road 1 km later.

- The road continues straight for 1 km passing long mounds with tall beech trees – glacial deposits. Nearest of these to the road is Dun an Oir with a rectangular stone structure on top: this is the burial ground of the Campbells of Glendaruel.

- From here, the road rises gently for 500 m, passing a medieval fortification on the right at the summit.

- The road descends through coppiced hazel, then crosses a burn before Achanelid Farm. The road gradually drops down to the valley floor and after 1·6 km crosses a cattle grid. Just beyond the grid there's an optional side-trip to Kildalvan's scattered ruins: see panel.

- Continue north-east along the road, passing another cattle grid after 1·3 km. Within 150 m you pass a traditional stone barn on your right with long ventilation strips.

> **i** **Kildalvan**
> To look for these ruins, follow the track that climbs the hill to your left. Glendaruel has the remains of several settlements, all long-deserted. Most were abandoned during the clearances following the Battle of Culloden (1746), and the population of Glendaruel never recovered. The remains of Kildalvan burial ground, with possible chapel, lie 350 m to the north-east. The round trip will take about an hour.

South over Glendaruel, winter sunrise

After 200 m, ignore the left fork to Kilbridemore Farm and proceed for another 300 m before crossing the bridge over the Kilbridemore Burn. Within 500 m you reach the junction with the A886.

For the side-trip to the Dunans Castle Heritage Trail, turn left and walk uphill for 400 m to the estate entrance on the right: see panel. To continue the Way, turn right and follow the road for 750 m to Garvie Farm.

 Dunans Castle Heritage Trail
*This is a circular walk through a woodland garden with its origins in a 17th century estate. Points of interest include the unique A-listed Telford Bridge, a fine collection of rhododendrons, rare native wildflowers, wild fungi, ancient trees and some stunning ravine views. The ruins of Dunans Castle are visible at the heart of the walk, though inaccessible: see **www.dunans.org**.*

At Garvie Farm, turn left to follow the farm road alongside a stone wall, with farm buildings to its left. After two gates, the track emerges into rough pasture.

After 500 m and another gate, the track begins to climb steadily by a series of bends, levelling out after passing under the power lines.

Continue downhill, ignoring a track that joins from the right, to a bridge over the Leth Allt. Follow the track uphill for 500 m to cross a gate-stile leading into the forest. Look behind you for good views to the south-west.

Continue uphill beside the Eas Davain burn, which tumbles over waterfalls. Walk through partly cleared forestry plantation for nearly 2 km to a crossroads, where you go straight over.

The track now swings right, after 150 m passing a disused sheep pen on your left and the fenced enclosure of Tom a' Chromain on your right.

The track heads gently uphill for 1 km, then rises more steeply. After 500 m you may see a small series of cascades on the Eas Davain above.

North over Glendaruel, late evening

Allt Robuic falls

- After another 400 m the track becomes less steep and a view may open up along the line of a fence to Beinn Bhuidhe (948 m), an isolated mountain over 25 km away at the head of Loch Fyne. Continue uphill to the highest point of this section.

- Continue downhill for about 1·5 km, ignoring the forest road that joins from the left. After a further 1·5 km and a series of bends, turn sharp left down the marked track on the left.

- After 400 m, where the track levels out, turn right by a small stream on to a narrow path through the trees.

- Follow the path for 100 m to emerge at a fence above the Allt Robuic gorge opposite one of many waterfalls.

- Turn left and follow the path down to cross the burn over a wooden bridge.

- Follow the path with yellow markers down the western side of the gorge, crossing above another waterfall after 80 m. After another 120 m, a short path to the right leads to a viewing platform beside a 25-metre fall.

- Continue downhill to a marked fork to your left. Ignore this, instead following blue markers to descend a flight of 40 steps. Continue for 100 m to meet the forest road.

- Turn left and follow the road, keeping the Glenshellish burn on your right. After 2 km, before reaching the 1950s forestry village to your left, you reach the Forestry Commission's District Office at Glenbranter. Local walks include the 'Lauder Walks', named after Sir Harry Lauder, the Edwardian entertainer who owned Glenbranter House.

- From here, follow the curve of the road to meet a junction beyond the sandstone entrance pillars. Turn left and follow the quiet road for 4 km to its junction with the A815 just south-east of Strachur village.

Old bridge over Glenshellish burn, Glenbranter

Strachur

Strachur, on the east shore of Loch Fyne, derives its name from strath (*valley*) and the River Cur (*heron*). The valley leads south-east along Loch Eck to the Clyde, and at one time the southern end of the parish formed the border between the ancient kingdoms of Dalriada and Strathclyde. Strachur was the traditional home of the Fergusson clan, but in more recent times it became a stronghold of the Campbells. The heart of the village lies half a mile inland from Loch Fyne, where you will find the traditional Clachan Inn and the Smiddy Museum: see panel. Here too is the Parish Church, which dates from 1709 and is beautifully situated within an oval churchyard. Set into the walls are a number of grave slabs dating back to the 14th century.

Nearer the shore is Strachur House, built by Sir John Campbell in the 1780s. This is now the family home of the late Sir Fitzroy Maclean, upon whom Ian Fleming allegedly based James Bond. A woodland walk through the grounds gives good views over Loch Fyne, and the flower gardens are occasionally open to the public in summer.

> **Strachur Smiddy Museum**
>
> The Smiddy (blacksmith's workshop) was first recorded in 1791. It played its vital role in the life of the local community until it closed in the 1950s. For most of its working life it was run by the Montgomery family, who provided four generations of village blacksmiths. After its closure, the Smiddy remained untouched for years.
>
> The Trust was set up in 1994 and local fund-raising helped to restore the building as a unique record of the blacksmith's craft.
>
> The Smiddy is open as a museum and craft shop from Easter to September. Hours are normally 1-4 pm (tel 01369 860 508).

Looking north across Strachur Bay

3·4 Strachur to Lochgoilhead

Distance	**8·7 miles 14·0 km**
Terrain	**quiet road, then farm and forest tracks, followed by rough ground with final 5 km of forest track and road**
Grade	**moderate climb to 350 m (1150 ft), then steepish descent**
Food and drink	**Strachur (hotel, pub, tearoom, shops), Lochgoilhead (hotels, shops)**
Summary	**quiet road followed by open hillside with rugged scenery and a remote lochan; fine views on the descent past Sruth Ban falls**

Strachur ——— — — — — — — — Curra Lochain — — — — — — — Lochgoilhead

4·7/7·6 4·0/6·4

- From the Glenbranter road junction, the Way crosses the A815 diagonally to the right.

- Go up the minor road opposite, which after 250 m turns right. Continue for 500 m, then turn left up the road signed for Succoth Farm.

- Follow the road uphill for 500 m to a cattle grid. From here the road goes downhill through woodland. Ignore the forest track that bears off left after 1 km, and continue a further 150 m to cross the road bridge over the River Cur.

- Once across the river, bear right to cross a second bridge over a burn.

- Go straight along a mossy track that enters the forest via a gate-stile. The forest road ascends steadily at first, with gradient easing later.

- After 1 km, bear right at a fork and continue uphill for 1 km to a T- junction: turn left.

Looking down toward Strachur from the forest road

- After 100 m, turn left along a forest road that snakes uphill. Follow this through felled forest for over 1 km to its end.
- A rough 4x4 track continues for 100 m to a fence and gate. Once through the gate, keep the fence to your right and follow the track for 250 m to its end.
- Bear left, crossing the tussocks, to reach the Leavanin burn. Turn right and follow the burn for 100 m before seeking the best spot to cross it. If in doubt, go higher.
- Once across the burn, head for the trees, turning right before you reach them, to pick up a faint 4x4 track.

- Before the forest descends to the burn, turn left into a wide ride that leads uphill for 100 m to a fence above the forest. At the top of the ride and to its right, there's a stile with waymarker (pictured).
- After the stile, turn right along the open hillside, keeping the fence on your right. There are white marker posts at intervals, but the ground near the fence can be very boggy. Taking a higher, parallel route may keep your feet drier.

Stile at top of forest ride

- After 300 m you pass a sheep pen above the bealach (pass) and glimpse the water of Curra Lochain ahead. Continue straight ahead, passing along the lochan's left shore, stepping over many feeder burns with cascades.

Curra Lochain

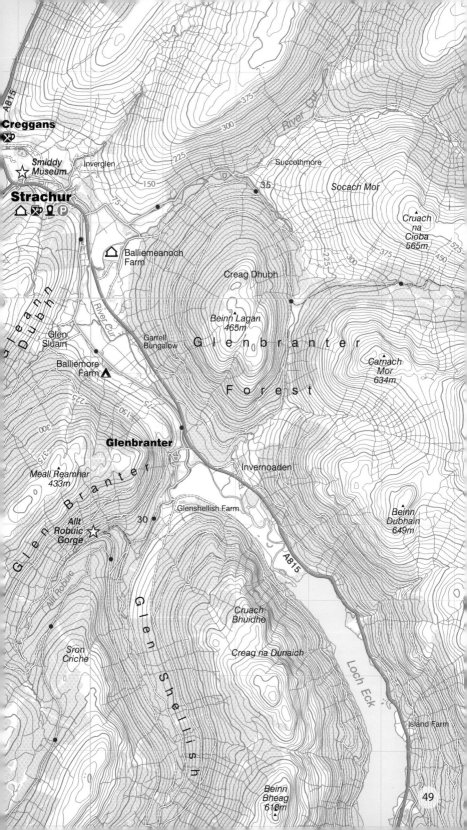

Creggans

Smiddy Museum

Inverglen

Strachur

Balliemeanoch Farm

Gleann Dubh

Glen Sluain

Balliemore Farm

Garrell Bungalow

Meall Reamhar
433m

Glenbranter

Allt Robuic Gorge

Glen Branter

Sron Criche

Glenshellish Farm

30

Succothmore

Socach Mor

Cruach na Cioba
565m

Creag Dhubh

Beinn Lagan
465m

Glenbranter

Forest

Carnach Mor
634m

Invernoaden

Beinn Dubhain
649m

Glen Shellish

Cruach Bhuidhe

Creag na Dunaich

Loch Eck

Island Farm

Beinn Bheag
618m

River Cur

375

300

225

150

75

35

35

225

300

375

450

525

225

150

75

300

375

225

150

A815

A815

- Take extra care at the lochan's far end, where the ground is broken. Choose carefully where to cross the outflow burn, especially when in spate. About 170 m beyond the stile, look for a large sloping boulder mid-stream that may help.

- If the burn is too high to cross safely, instead stay on the left side and carefully descend the hillside to the forest road at the bottom of the glen, bypassing the falls to reach the timber bridge mentioned at the top of page 52.

- Otherwise, once across turn left and follow the fence line down the glen on an often-sodden path.

- After 300 m, a steep drop begins to the lower glen, with the Sruth Ban series of waterfalls to your left and views of Lochgoilhead in the distance. The path swings away to the right, then back beneath the main fall, as confirmed by white marker posts.

Patch of forest below Sruth Ban falls

- From here look for a gap in the patch of forest about 100 m below: see the photographs above and on page 52. Descend to this gap and walk through the trees.

Sruth Ban falls

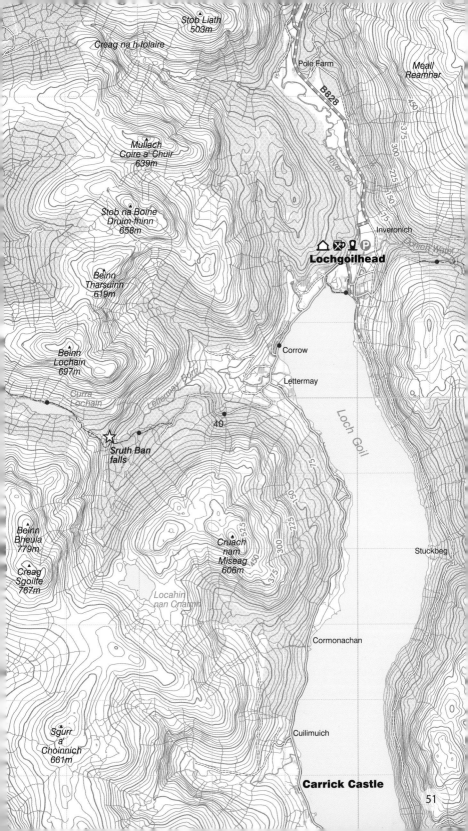

Stob Liath
503m

Creag na h-Iolaire

Meall
Reamhar

Pole Farm

B828

River Goil

Mullach
Coire a' Chuir
639m

Inveronich

Donich Water

Lochgoilhead

Stob na Boine
Druim-fhinn
658m

Beinn
Tharsuinn
619m

Beinn
Lochain
697m

Corrow

Curra
Lochain

Lettermay

Lettermay Burn

Loch Goil

Sruth Ban
falls

Beinn
Bheula
779m

Cruach
nam
Miseag
606m

Stuckbeg

Creag
Sgoilte
767m

Locahin
nan Cnamh

Cormonachan

Sgurr
a'
Choinnich
661m

Cuilimuich

Carrick Castle

- Within 100 m you reach a forest road, where you turn right and cross a timber bridge (to the right of the stone bridge at the centre of the photograph below).

- Follow the road to a junction, where you veer left and follow the road downhill, ignoring a smaller track that soon bears off left.

- Continue downhill for a total of about 2 km to a forest gate. Beyond it, the track descends to meet the public road within 500 m.

- Turn left along the road for 2 km past the estate of timber chalets and static caravans, towards the head of Loch Goil. To reach the village centre, if the tide is low, take the footbridge over the River Goil and follow the embanked footpath and then the beach. If the tide is high, follow the road to its junction with the B839, and turn right.

Patch of forest seen from Sruth Ban falls

Lochgoilhead

Lochgoilhead enjoys a fine situation at the head of Loch Goil, a steep-sided sea loch that forms an inlet of Loch Long – itself an arm of the Firth of Clyde: see the title page photograph. Road access to the village is by one of two single-track roads through mountainous terrain. The first is a spectacular 6-mile stretch from the top of the *Rest and be Thankful* pass; the second is the approach from Loch Fyne, aptly named *Hell's Glen*.

Lochgoilhead has been Glasgow's 'lung' for at least 150 years. The village developed greatly after the coming of the Clyde steamers. In the 19th century, the merchant princes built a row of villas to the south of the village, and commuted from here to Glasgow. Ardgoil Estate, the hilly area between Lochs Goil and Long, was in 1905 gifted to Glasgow City for the benefit and enjoyment of its citizens.

The Lochgoilhead and Kilmorich parish Church is one of the oldest foundations in Cowal. The present building dates from the 18th century but probably includes most of an earlier church built in 1379. Its graveyard has some grandiose monuments. One bears a long eulogy to Archibald Campbell of Drimsynie, in marked contrast to the simple inscription to his wife.

> *i*
> **Drimsynie House**
> built in the 1850s by James Neilson, the Glasgow engineer who patented the blast furnace. It was later owned by the Livingstone family whose crest and motto remains above the original entrance. It was opened as a hotel in 1958, later bought by the Campbells, who added a leisure centre. The ranks of chalets in its former grounds are home to thousands of holiday-makers who come from the central belt to enjoy 'the Highlands'.

Drimsynie House, original entrance

3·5 Lochgoilhead to Inveruglas

Distance	15·0 miles 24·1 km
Terrain	quiet road, then farm and forest tracks, followed by rough ground with final 5 km of forest track and road
Grade	strenuous climb to 500 m (1640 ft), followed by steep descent at first on path, then forest road; two further lesser ascents
Food and drink	Lochgoilhead (hotels, shops), Arrochar (hotels, pubs, shops), Inveruglas (café)
Summary	stiff climb to the pass is rewarded by great views in clear weather; after scenic Loch Long, pleasant walk through Glen Loin leads to journey's end at Loch Lomond

Lochgoilhead — Cairn — Ardgartan — Arrochar — Inveruglas

2·6 /4·2   3·5 /5·6   3·1 /5·0   5·8 /9·3

- From the village centre, head east up the road signed for the public toilets, just left of the Post Office and shop. Continue to its end, then along a path through the trees.

- Emerging from the trees, cross a gate-stile and continue uphill to an electricity pole. Turn left, then take the uphill of two vehicle tracks through another gate-stile with a post signed 'Donich Circular 4 km'.

East over Lochgoilhead, with Cobbler (left) and Brack (right)

- Follow the stony road (with Lochgoilhead Arboretum to its left) uphill for 1 km through a gate-stile. Afterwards continue for 400 m, and cross a footbridge.

- Bear right as marked by the post 'Coilessan Hill Walk'. This forges uphill, steeply at first, soon reaching a huge boulder: see the photograph on page 20.

- Turn right up the wide, steep ride just after the boulder. Keep to the right of the burn, following the rough traces of a boggy path.

- The path deteriorates but continues uphill, past a junction marked 'Glen Croe'. Near the top of the ride, the Way veers right over boggy ground to a stile in the fence.

- From this point the Way heads easterly across 1·5 km of open hill to the cairn shown below. This is at GR 234 019, just beyond the Way's highest point (500 m/1640 ft). Widely spaced white marker posts lead to the cairn, but the path is ill-defined.

- In poor visibility, use your map and compass: from the stile, follow 71° for 600 m to a marker post raised on a mound; then follow 88° for 550 m to the cairn; finally follow 100° for 230 m to the gate-stile. (These magnetic bearings were valid in 2015.)

- In clear conditions, simply cross the stile and follow the white markers which lead across a shallow basin (with a small lochan on its left) to the cairn shown below. At this altitude, the snow in this photograph is unusual, even in mid-winter.

- There may be spectacular views ahead to the Luss Hills, with Ben Lomond beyond. Behind are good views to Beinn Bheula (see photo overleaf), whilst to the left is the Brack.

North-east from the cairn, with Ben Lomond distant at the right

West from the summit cairn, toward Beinn Bheula

- From the cairn, continue downhill for about 250 m across the hillside to enter the forest at a gate-stile. If in doubt, look north-east from the cairn for a fence and simply follow its line downhill to the gate-stile.

- After crossing the fence, take the quad bike track steeply downhill through the forest, and bear right down the forest road.

- After a further 850 m, bear right again at the fork. Continue downhill for 450 m to cross the Coilessan Burn by concrete bridge.

- Continue downhill for a further 650 m to a T-junction. Turn hard left for 200 m, re-crossing the burn and passing through the forestry barrier on to a tarmac road.

- Follow this quiet, but public, road for 1·5 km. Look out for March Cottage on the right, and after a further 400 m, bear right down a small path that descends to the shore of Loch Long.

- The lochside path takes you to the imposing Ardgartan Hotel. Take the road leading away from the hotel.

- Continue along this tarmac road until you pass Ardgartan Lodge.

Ardgartan Hotel

- Turn right across the timber bridge, then immediately left, following waymarkers to a junction about 300 m short of Ardgartan picnic site. To continue the Way direct to Arrochar, bear right (yellow marker) up the cycle track and cross the busy A83.

- The picnic site is worth visiting if you have time. Located beside the Croe Water, this is a popular stop for walkers, cyclists and motorists. The information boards in the car park provide maps, and there are picnic benches and public toilets. Afterwards, retrace your steps to the yellow marker to resume the Way.

- The cycleway climbs steadily to join an old forestry track. Views across Loch Long to Ben Reoch appear between the trees to your right.

- The track joins a forest road and continues north-east, about 2 km from Ardgartan passing a radio mast on your right. The Cobbler ascent turns left here: see page 59.

- Continue for 100 m and bear right down the steep path that zigzags to the loch-side.

- To continue the Way to Inveruglas, skip to page 62. For the shops and facilities of Arrochar, follow the A83 pavement for 400 m into the village centre. Or, if you have to terminate your walk at Arrochar, refer to the foot of page 60.

North-west down the cycleway above Ardgartan

Arrochar from the head of Loch Long

Arrochar

Arrochar sits at the head of Loch Long, a long thin finger of the Clyde estuary. The A83 runs through the village, and is the gateway to both Cowal and Kintyre. Only a couple of miles to its east lies Tarbet on the fresh water of Loch Lomond, with its modern road and rail connections to Glasgow and the north.

The narrow valley joining the two lochs has been of strategic importance since Viking times. It was short enough to be a portage route for boats, and in 1263 the Viking raiders hauled their long-ships across it to Tarbet, to raid the shores of Loch Lomond.

Arrochar is surrounded by spectacular mountains including four Munros (mountains over 3000 feet/914 m) that attract many walkers and climbers. Known affectionately as the Arrochar Alps, this group also contains the Cobbler – a magnet for climbers year-round. Its special place in Scottish rock climbing was celebrated by the formation in 1863 of the Cobbler Club, Scotland's first climbing group.

The Cobbler falls just short of Munro height, but its craggy summit and magnificent views more than compensate. Officially 'Ben Arthur', it has long been better known by its nickname, and was referred to thus by William and Dorothy Wordsworth (1803). The image is of a cobbler (north and central peaks) hunched over his wife (southern peak).

Climbing the Cobbler (2890 ft /881 m)

Allow 4-6 hours for this 8-mile round trip from sea level. Give yourself time to enjoy the summit views and a margin of daylight for safety: it's a strenuous climb with some tricky terrain. In low cloud or bad weather, don't attempt it unless you are experienced and properly equipped for the conditions. Although you could begin your ascent direct from the Cowal Way (see page 58, bullet 4), adding this climb to section 3·5 would make for a very long and challenging day, strictly for the energetic climber with plenty of daylight in hand and confident of good conditions.

East toward Ben Lomond from the Cobbler

From the car park west of Arrochar (see map below), cross the A83 to the timber vehicle barrier and follow the sign 'Ben Narnain and Cobbler'. A well-made path zigzags uphill to a forestry road, part of the Cowal Way. Turn left towards the communications mast, then fork right uphill, just in front of it.

Climb steadily by the zigzags to reach the Buttermilk Burn just above its small

Over Loch Long from beside the Cobbler's summit

intake dam. This is the nearly-halfway point, and now you can see your goal with its three rugged peaks.

Follow the clear path upstream to the two huge Narnain Boulders, prominent glacial remnants. About 300 m above them, turn left at the path junction toward the East Corrie. Cross the stream and take the steep, rugged path to the col between central and north peaks. From here, the north peak (up right) is an easy scramble, or you can turn up left to the gravel dome beside the central peak (the summit).

Attaining the summit requires rock-climbing skills to 'thread the needle' and scramble along a narrow, exposed ledge: see photograph above. In wet conditions, this is downright dangerous. Most walkers settle for the superb panorama from just below, looking over Lochs Long and Lomond, the Firth of Clyde and the islands of Bute and Arran.

Away from Arrochar

You can leave Arrochar by Citylink bus, or, if you prefer the train, take the pleasant woodland walk that contours the lower slopes of Cruaich Tairbeart above the road. Go up the steps by the village phone box, and at the T-junction turn right to follow the Cruaich Tairbeart yellow markers through birch and oak woodland. Within 1·5 km you reach a well-marked junction, where you bear right down a short path to the station: access to the platform is via the tunnel.

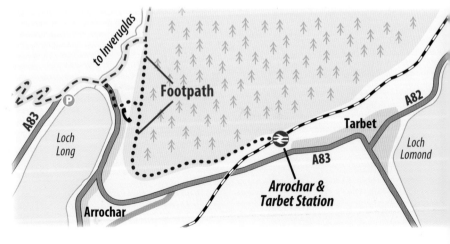

Inveruglas

An Ceann Mor

Inversnaid

Coiregrogain

Inveruglas Water

55

Dubh Chnoc

Kenmore Wood

A' Chrois
849m

Creag
Tharsuinn

Glen Loin

Loin Water

Blairannaich

Cailne

Loch Lomond

Feorlinn

Cruach
Tairbeirt
415m

Succoth

Arrochar & Tarbet

Tarbet

Rowchoish

Loch Long

A83

50

Arrochar

rdgartan

Ardmay

Ben Reoch
661m

Hollybank

West Highland Way

Firkin
Toll
Cottage

An t-Sreang

Firkin
Point

Tullich Hill
632m

Water Bus - seasonal

61

Arrochar to Inveruglas

- Locate the bridge over the Loin Water at the head of Loch Long (north of Arrochar village centre). Head north up Glen Loin on the marked forest track, with the river on your left.

- After 200 m, before the farmhouse, turn right at the 'Stronafyne Loop Walk' sign. Follow this path which curves uphill for 150 m, then turn left at the T-junction with the forest track. (A right turn here would take you along the path toward the station, see previous page.)

- After 1 km of shaded track, pass through a kissing-gate. The path is bordered by bog myrtle, and heads north over open ground, across a timber footbridge and through another kissing-gate.

- The path continues northerly uphill, parallel to the lines of pylons, and climbs steeply under the pylons to a rocky outcrop. It then dips and rises to a viewpoint at 150 m.

Path through Glen Loin

Rocky outcrop below viewpoint

- The path descends to cross a short plateau before bearing left, at first alongside, then through, conifer forest. Soon you start seeing Loch Lomond to your right, and the Loch Sloy road heading eastward towards it on the far side of the valley.

- Descend to the timber bridge and cross Inveruglas Water. Turn right up the path that soon meets the Sloy road: turn right, descending the valley toward Loch Lomond.

- Follow this tarmac private road downhill for nearly 2 km, past the electricity sub-station. Enjoy fine views across the loch to Ben Lomond and Inversnaid.

- Descend to pass under the railway viaduct (the West Highland Line). At the busy A82 road, turn left

Pipelines to Sloy Power Station

to follow the roadside path for 800 m. Just after Sloy Power Station, you reach Inveruglas, where there's a Visitor Centre with toilets and picnic site.

- Be sure to climb the 8-metre timber pyramid above the jetty which marks the Cowal Way terminus. Its name *An Ceann Mor* (Gaelic for 'large headland') describes its location, and there are outstanding views over Loch Lomond from its platform.

The Water Bus may take you across the loch from here to Inversnaid, but only in season and if pre-booked: see page 70. Or there's a Scottish Citylink bus south to Glasgow or north to Ardlui. There's a small café at the jetty where you can celebrate your completion of the Way.

An Ceann Mor viewpoint, Inveruglas

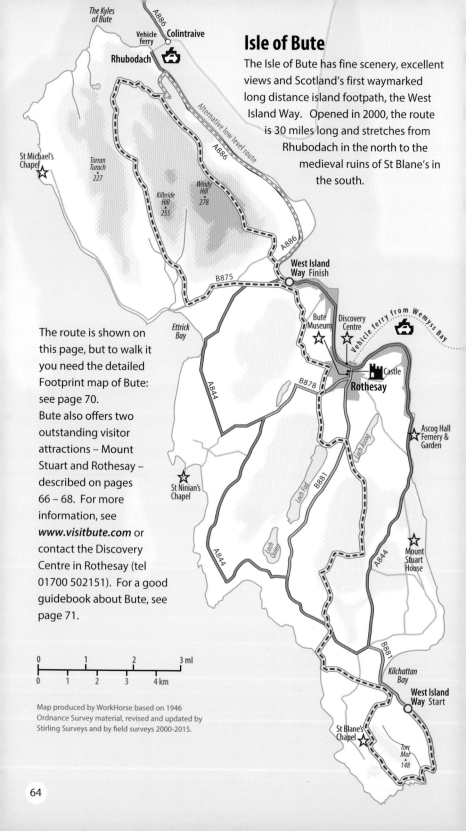

Isle of Bute

The Isle of Bute has fine scenery, excellent views and Scotland's first waymarked long distance island footpath, the West Island Way.   Opened in 2000, the route is 30 miles long and stretches from Rhubodach in the north to the medieval ruins of St Blane's in the south.

The route is shown on this page, but to walk it you need the detailed Footprint map of Bute: see page 70. Bute also offers two outstanding visitor attractions – Mount Stuart and Rothesay – described on pages 66 – 68. For more information, see *www.visitbute.com* or contact the Discovery Centre in Rothesay (tel 01700 502151). For a good guidebook about Bute, see page 71.

The Kyles of Bute

Colintraive
Vehicle ferry
Rhubodach

A886

St Michael's Chapel

Torran Turach 227

Kilbride Hill 255

Windy Hill 278

Alternative low level route

A886

B875

West Island Way Finish

Ettrick Bay

Bute Museum

Discovery Centre

Vehicle ferry from Wemyss Bay

Castle
Rothesay

B878

A844

St Ninian's Chapel

Loch Fad

Loch Quien

Loch Ascog

B881

Ascog Hall Fernery & Garden

Mount Stuart House

A844

B881

Kilchattan Bay

West Island Way Start

St Blane's Chapel

Torr Mor 148

Map produced by WorkHorse based on 1946 Ordnance Survey material, revised and updated by Stirling Surveys and by field surveys 2000-2015.

0   1   2   3 ml
0 1 2 3 4 km

Getting to and from Bute

Wemyss Bay, the terminal for the Rothesay ferry, can be reached by train from Glasgow Central, and the crossing to Rothesay takes about 35 minutes. Sailings leave at least hourly year-round, more often in summer. The Colintraive ferry runs frequently, also year-round, with a 5-minutes crossing and only a 5-minute check-in time. From Rhubodach, walkers can reach Rothesay by bus or on foot. For ferry details, contact CalMac: see page 70.

Colintraive is Cowal's gateway to Bute. Cowal Way walkers can make the side-trip by leaving the Way at Glendaruel. Public transport to the quiet village of Colintraive is sparse and travel should be planned in advance. On foot, the walk from Glendaruel is about 8 miles/13 km, with its first part on main road. Thereafter take the little-used coastal road that winds through woods and over headlands, gradually revealing the beauty of the Kyles of Bute.

In summer, the world's oldest ocean-going paddle steamer, the Waverley, can be seen ploughing through these narrows. Colintraive means *the narrows of the swimming* and this is where drovers sent their cattle swimming across from Bute on their way to mainland markets. The straits are only about 200 m (650 ft) wide at their narrowest point. There's a quiet hotel by the slipway.

Ferry leaving Rhubodach for Colintraive

Mount Stuart

The present Mount Stuart is a Victorian gothic fantasy, the size of a small palace. It's the creation of John Patrick Crichton-Stuart, third Marquess of Bute, and his architect, Sir Robert Rowand Anderson.

The Marquess was reputed to be the richest man in Britain. He was also one of those extraordinary Victorians of inexhaustible energy and talent; a scholar, speaker of a dozen languages or more, and a major patron of the arts.

When the old Mount Stuart was seriously damaged by fire in 1877, he seized the opportunity to build an immensely ambitious new stately home. Its construction continued over the next hundred years.

Great hall

Horoscope room

Mount Stuart is open to the public daily from Easter to the end of October, subject to special events: check ***www.mountstuart.com*** or phone 01700 503 877 to confirm. Visitors can marvel at the great hall, higher than many cathedrals and the white marble chapel. The Third Marquess's private sitting room (now known as the 'horoscope room') has an amazing ceiling showing the position of the planets at the hour of his birth on 12 September 1847.

The main public rooms contain a fine array of furnishings and a world class collection of paintings. The house is surrounded by extensive gardens with a magnificent botanic collection from around the world. There are beautiful beaches and woodland walks: visit ***www.mountstuart.com***.

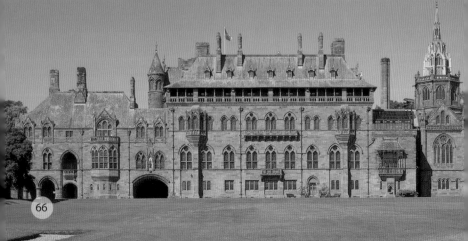

Rothesay

Rothesay is the only large town on Bute, with over 80% of the Island's population of 6700. It was Scotland's first Royal Burgh with its Charter granted in 1401 by King Robert III. Its rich history is interwoven with that of the Stuart family, but what the visitor sees today is a small seaside resort with palm trees and beautifully tended gardens.

Rothesay has an excellent collection of Victorian architecture of every sort. It must be unique in featuring a public lavatory high in its list of attractions – but the lavishly tiled gents toilet at the Pier is a Victorian masterpiece dating from 1889. Female visitors are encouraged to admire its facilities whenever they are not in active use.

Glorious Victorian plumbing

The Waverley at Rothesay Pier

The Winter Gardens on the promenade date from 1924 and have been restored; they house a modern cinema and the Discovery Centre (with visitor information). The nearby Rothesay Pavilion, built in 1938 in international style, is an outstanding example of early leisure architecture. The Bute Museum (next to the castle) covers the island's natural and human heritage; it is run by enthusiastic and talented volunteers.

Rothesay Pavilion

Rothesay's history is closely connected with its unique, large circular castle. Rothesay Castle may have begun with the Vikings in the 11th century, when they controlled most of the Scottish islands. Although torched by the Duke of Argyll's soldiers in 1685 and reduced to ruins until 1816, enough is restored and visible today to let your imagination summon those distant times. It is maintained by Historic Scotland and is open year-round: tel 01700 502691.

Rothesay Castle

5 Reference

Origin of the Cowal Way

The Cowal Way was created and developed by James McLuckie, a resident of Glendaruel since 1986 and co-author of this book. From his initial idea of a simple long-distance footpath, the route developed into a history and heritage trail. With support from the Colintraive and Glendaruel Community Council and with National Lottery funding, establishing the Way became a Millennium project.

With further support from Argyll and Bute Council, the first guidebook was published in 2001 and the Cowal Way officially opened in May 2003. Initially, the Way was established to keep open some of the traditional cross-country routes and rights of way. In 2009 the route was extended from Ardgartan to Inveruglas, making the route also link with the Kintyre Way and the West Highland Way. The first Rucksack Reader guidebook documented the extended route, and this 2016 edition is an updated version of that guidebook, enhanced by large-scale Footprint mapping.

In 2015, Colintraive and Glendaruel Development Trust, which has managed the Way since 2012, secured funding from the Coastal Communiities Fund to upgrade the whole route with the goal of recognition as one of Scotland's Great Trails by 2016-17.

Supporters

The authors wish to thank the following agencies for their continuing support: the Forestry Commission Scotland, for guidance and advice on route selection, and for prompt effective maintenance:
  www.forestry.gov.uk/argyllforestpark

Argyll and Bute Council:
  www.argyll-bute.gov.uk
Highlands and Islands Enterprise*:*
  www.hie.co.uk
Loch Lomond and the Trossachs National Park:
  www.lochlomond-trossachs.org
Scottish Natural Heritage:
  www.snh.gov.uk

For more on the *Scottish Outdoor Access Code*, visit *www.outdooraccess-scotland.com*. You can download a leaflet about SOAC from *www.snh.gov.uk/docs/B621366.pdf* and the useful *Dog Owners* leaflet from *www.snh.gov.uk/docs/C233791.pdf*

Useful websites

Visit the official website for this route both when planning your trip and before setting out, in case of any route updates. Its interactive map helps you to find accommodation and food:
  www.cowalway.co.uk
Many other useful links are provided at
  www.rucsacs.com/links/cly

Visitor Information Centres

The only Visitor Information Centre in Cowal is in Dunoon: 01369 703 785. Others are at Balloch (for Loch Lomond and the Trossachs) 01389 753 533; Tarbert, Loch Fyne (for Kintyre, seasonal) 01880 820 429; Discovery Centre, Rothesay (for Bute) 01700 502 151.

Emergencies

In an emergency, dial 999 and be ready to state the problem, location and number of people affected. The operator will connect you to police, ambulance or fire service, and if appropriate may also call out mountain rescue or coastguard services.

Weather

Weather information is available on various websites, but be aware that Cowal's weather is very localised and changeable:

www.metoffice.com
www.bbc.co.uk/weather
www.mwis.org

Tide tables

Tidal information is available in local time, free and far in the future, at

www.tides4fishing.com/uk/scotland/ rothesay-bay

Public transport

Traveline Scotland (for public transport in Scotland)   0871 200 2233

www.travelinescotland.com
ScotRail (Scotland's railway)

www.scotrail.co.uk

Ferries

Argyll Ferries (Gourock station to Dunoon, foot passengers)

0800 066 5000 *www.argyllferries.co.uk*

Calmac Ferries (for Arran, Bute, Kintyre and other ferries)

0800 066 5000 *www.calmac.co.uk*

Loch Lomond Water Bus services are seasonal and timings vary: there's an on demand service from Inveruglas to Inversnaid from late March to end October:

www.lochlomond-trossachs.org/waterbus

This *must* be pre-booked, phone ahead on 01301 702 356.

Western Ferries (vehicle ferry to Dunoon from Gourock) 01369 704 452

www.western-ferries.co.uk

Buses

Scottish Citylink (Scottish buses)

0871 266 3333 *www.citylink.co.uk*

West Coast Motors (covers Cowal, Bute and Kintyre) 01586 552 319

www.westcoastmotors.co.uk

Airlines

British Airways	*www.ba.com*
easyJet	*www.easyJet.com*
Ryanair	*www.ryanair.com*

Baggage handling

A dedicated baggage handling service is scheduled to start in 2016: see

www.cowalway.co.uk for updates.

Maps (printed and online)

The Ordnance Survey Explorer maps spread Cowal over three maps (from south to north, sheets 362, 363 and 364) at a scale of 1:25,000, with the Way marked by green lozenges. As of 2016, the section from Ardgartan to Inveruglas was not marked, but its area was covered.

For walking the West Island Way we recommend the Footprint map *Discover the Isle of Bute* (978-1-871149-82-1) which maps the whole island at large scale (1:30,000) and includes West Island Way route notes. Its price in 2016 was £6.95.

Please visit our online route map at

www.rucsacs.com/routemap/cly

and zoom in for amazing detail. It shows the route very accurately as an overlay on Google maps, and you can use it to search for accommodation and refreshments near the route.

Further reading

Woods, L and Vickers, D (2013)

Cowal & Bute: the Guide Book

Aird Trading, 978-0-95621266-5

Compact and up-to-date guidebook covering heritage and attractions, with plenty of photographs 72pp

Paterson, Bridget (2004) *Colintraive and Glendaruel: a Small Country.* Birlinn, 978-1-84158-400-3

A meticulously researched but very readable history of the area by a local author with an intimate knowledge of the land and the people.

Bailey, Patrick (2007) *The Isle of Bute*
Pevensey Island Guides
978-0715334-94-2
Well-written and with many photographs, this is a good source on the island's heritage, landscape, flora and fauna.

Acknowledgements

The authors thank all those who assisted with research and commented on drafts: Charlie Collins, Annie Craig, Elizabeth Fairbairn, Fiona Hamilton, Anne Lamb, Kate McEwan, Martin McFarlane, Kirsty McLuckie, Stewart Miller, Margaret Shields and Don Williams; and the publisher warmly thanks Rob and Di Tennent for support and Lindsay Merriman for proof-reading. Their efforts led to many improvements, but any remaining flaws are our responsibility. We welcome feedback, preferably by email to: **info@rucsacs.com.**

Notes for novices

Advice for novices on choosing and using walking gear, and on daily distances, is provided at *www.rucsacs.com*.

Photo credits

Charlie Collins 38 (upper), 48, 57 (lower); **Drimsynie House Hotel** 53; **Forestry Commission Scotland** 11, 21, 25 (upper), 29 (lower); **Michael Kaufmann** back cover, 5 (lower), 7 (lower), 12 (upper), 17 (lower), 19 (upper), 26 (lower), 36, 40 (both), 41, 47, 50 (lower), 52; **Michael McGurk** 62-3 (lower), 63 (upper); **James McLuckie** 4, 6, 10, 11, 12 (lower), 19 (upper), 22, 26 (lower), 30, 32 (lower), 34, 38 (lower), 42, 45, 46, 50 (upper), 54, 63; **Jacquetta Megarry** 5 (upper), 7 (upper), 13 (upper), 16, 18, 20 (lower), 24 (upper), 31 (both), 32 (upper), 38 (middle), 56, 57 (upper), 58 (lower), 59, 60, 62 (upper two), 65; **Stewart Miller** 11; **Sandy Morrison** 26 (upper), 28 (lower); **Mount Stuart Trust** 66 (all); **Thomas Nugent** 67 (lower), 68 (upper); **John Openshaw** 14; www.CharliePhillipsimages.co.uk 24 (lower); ChrisSharratt.co.uk 25 (lower), 27 (upper); **Gordon Simm** 29 (upper); **Stuart Smith** 13 (lower); **Robert Tennent** 23, 58 (upper); **Ronald Turnbull** title page, 44, 45 (lower); **VisitScotland/Scottish Viewpoint** front cover; www.scran.ac.uk (licensor) for © **National Museums Scotland** 67 (upper) and © **Crown/Historic Scotland** 68 (lower).

Rucksack Readers® **Adventurous long-distance walks in Scotland**

Moray Coast Trail
Great Glen Way
West Highland Way
Cowal Way
Kintyre Way
Arran Coastal Way

Speyside Way
Cateran Trail
Rob Roy Way
Mary Queen of Scots Way
Fife Coastal Path
John Muir Way
St Cuthbert's Way

Forres, Cullen, Inverness, Dava Way, Grantown-on-Spey, Aviemore, Fort William, Pitlochry, Blairgowrie, Newburgh, St Andrews, Inveruglas, Kincardine, Dunbar, Portavadie, Drymen, Tarbert, Helensburgh, Lindisfarne, Brodick, Melrose, Machrihanish

For updates and news visit *www.rucsacs.com*

Index